Car Trouble

Story by Kathryn Sutherland

Illustrations by Rachel Tonkin

The bell rang loudly
at the end of the school day.
Children and parents were everywhere,
and cars came and went.

But when they had all gone,
Claire and her little brother, Lewis,
were still there, waiting for Dad.
He was late—again.

"Dad's probably had car trouble," said Lewis.
"Let's go back to the classroom
and wait with my teacher."

"No, let's wait here today," said Claire.
"Then we'll be able to see Dad coming."

Lewis wasn't sure that this was a good idea.
"But Miss Greco says we should wait with her
if our parents are late," he argued.

"It doesn't matter. Dad won't be long,"
said Claire. "We'll stand here by the gate."

Minutes later, a blue car
came around the corner.
"That's not Dad," said Lewis.

"No, but it looks like Aunt Jane's car,"
said Claire. "Maybe she's picking us up."

"That's not Aunt Jane in the car,"
said Lewis.

The car slowed down. The driver stared
at Claire and Lewis. Then she drove off.

Soon the same car came past again,
and this time it stopped.

The driver rolled the window down
and called to Claire and Lewis.
"Who are you waiting for?" she asked.

"Our dad," Lewis told her.

"Your dad asked me to pick you up,"
replied the woman.
"Get in and I'll drive you home."

Claire didn't like the sound of that.
She felt funny inside—uncomfortable.
Dad would never send a stranger
to pick them up.
But it was hard to say *no* to a grown-up.

Lewis picked up his backpack
and walked toward the woman's car.
Claire called out to him,
"No, Lewis! Come back here!"

He started to turn back,
but the woman spoke softly to him.
"Come on, honey.
You'll come with me, won't you?"

She opened the car door.

Lewis wasn't sure what to do.
He just wished that Dad would come.
He looked from the driver to Claire,
and back again.
He was about to go to the car
when Claire spoke to the woman
in a strong voice.

"No, thank you," she said.
"We'll both wait for our dad.
Come back, Lewis."

Lewis was confused.
"But the lady said
Dad wants us to go with her,"
he said to Claire.

"I think she's tricking us," said Claire.
"I'm sure Dad will come soon."

The driver suddenly became angry.
"Your dad asked me to take you home.
Now get in the car!" she yelled.

The children were very frightened,
but Claire knew she had to be brave.
She took a deep breath
and in a very loud voice said,
"**No!** We will go and wait with our teacher."

Claire grabbed Lewis by the hand
and pulled him toward her.
Then they ran back to the classroom,
feeling very scared.

Claire and Lewis were crying
as they told Miss Greco what had happened.

"I'm so glad you didn't get into that car,"
she said. "You were very sensible."

"But we should have come back here,
instead of waiting at the gate
by ourselves," said Claire.

"Yes," Miss Greco agreed.
"But if you can tell me
what the woman looked like,
that will be a big help.
I'll have to call the police,
because we don't want any other children
getting into that car."

"She had short brown hair," said Lewis.

"And a red scarf," said Claire.

Then their dad walked into the room.
"Sorry I'm late," he said.
"I had car trouble."

"We've had some car trouble, too,"
said Miss Greco.
"I was just going to call the police."

They told Dad all about
the strange woman in the blue car.

"Did you see the license plate?" Dad asked.

"No," said Claire.

"But the car was just the same
as Aunt Jane's car," said Lewis.

"Good," said Dad. "We can tell the police
exactly what it looked like,
and that will help them find the driver."

"It was very hard to say *no* to a grown-up,"
Claire told Dad.

"But you trusted your feelings," said Dad.
"You felt that something was wrong, Claire,
and you took care of Lewis.
You both did the right thing,
and I'm very proud of you."

"I'm going to get the car fixed tomorrow," said Dad.
"And then I won't be late again."

"Good," said Lewis.

"Yes," agreed Claire.
"We don't want any more car trouble."